Contents

Welcome to Amsterdam!

This opening fold-out contains four pages of valuable information, handy tips and useful addresses, and a general map of Amsterdam to help you visualise the six districts discussed in this guide. On the map, indicated by a star, are the ten sights not to be missed if your visit is a short one.

Discover Amsterdam through six districts and six maps

- **A** Centraal Station / Nieuwmarkt / Dam / Spui
- **B** Jordaan / Northern canals / Western islands
- **C** Southern canals / Leidseplein / Singel
- **D** Rembrandtplein / Amstel / Waterlooplein
- **E** Vondelpark / Museumplein / De Pijp
- **F** Plantage / Oosterdok / Zeeburg

For each district there is a double-page of addresses (restaurants – listed in ascending order of price – pubs, bars, music venues and shops) followed by a fold-out map for the relevant area with the essential places to see (indicated on the map by a star ★). These places are by no means all that Amsterdam has to offer but to us they are unmissable. The grid-referencing system (**A** B2) makes it easy to pinpoint addresses quickly on the map.

Transport and hotels in Amsterdam
The last fold-out consists of a transport map and four pages of practical information that include a selection of hotels.

Thematic index
Lists all the addresses, sites and monuments mentioned in this guide.

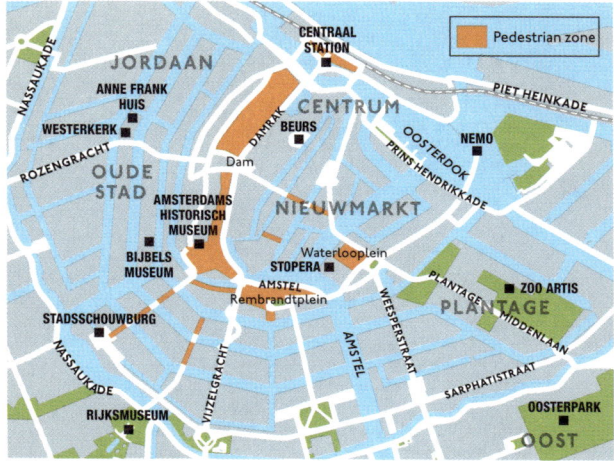
LANDMARKS IN THE CITY CENTER

→ *First weekend; Amstel, Prinsengracht, Stopera*
Techno music and parades on the canals.
Uitmarkt
→ *Last weekend; uitmarkt.nl*
Open-air shows.
Grachten Festival
→ *Five days; grachtenfestival.nl*
Classical music in concert halls, museums, parks, etc.

September-October
Jordaan Festival
→ *Mid-Sep, Jordaan jordaanfestival.nl*
Shows, dance, street performances, etc.
Open Monumentendag
→ *Second weekend in Oct; openmonumentendag.nl*
Access to listed buildings and monuments.
Marathon
→ *Third Sun in Oct*
From the Olympic Stadium to the River Amstel.

November-December
Museumnacht
→ *First Sat in Nov; n8.nl*
Museums open until 2am.
Cannabis Cup
→ *Third week in Nov, for five days; cannabiscup.com*
Prize for the best herb, the best coffeeshop, etc.
IDFA (Internationaal Documentaires Filmfestival Amsterdam)
→ *End of Nov, in several movie theaters; idfa.nl*
Part of the worldwide short film festival.
Sinterklaas
→ *Procession: first Sun after Nov 15; holiday: Dec 5-6*
Saint Nicholas arrives in the city: parades, distribution of candles.

MONEY

Budget
Accommodation
Around €80 for a bedroom en-suite, €60 with shared bathroom.
Restaurants
Always more expensive in the evening (main course €15–25). Reasonable prices in many cafés and delis. It is customary to leave a 5 percent tip, or round up the total. The prices include VAT.
Museums
Between €7 and €15.
Going out
Drinks and admission prices are fairly reasonable.
Credit cards
Cash dispensers are everywhere (streets, supermarkets, etc.), but be warned: payment by credit card is rarely accepted.

OPENING TIMES

Public holidays
→ *Restricted opening, with banks and official offices closed, along with most stores and museums.*
Restaurants
→ *Apart from delis (open approx. 9am-6pm) selling pre-prepared food and brasseries (11am-10pm), very*

ARCHITECTURE

Dutch Renaissance (16th–17th c.)
With red-brick façades, clocktowers and ornate gables, this is a very decorative style, with Hendrik de Keyser as its figurehead (1565–1621); **Bartolotti Huis** (**B** C5), **Westerkerk** (**B** B5)
Dutch classicism (17th c.)
The order, sobriety and geometry of the architectural lines recall Greco-Roman principles; Jacob Van Campen (1596–1657) and the Vingboons brothers: Justus (1620–98) and Philips (1607–78); **Koninklijk Paleis** (**A** A3)
Start of 20th century
Three styles: neo-Renaissance (end of the 19th century) with the **Centraal Station** (**A** C1); then Art Nouveau and Art Deco, with the **Tuschinski Theater** (**D** B2).
Amsterdam School (20th century)
Expressionnist style with widespread use of brickwork; Johan Van der Mey (1878-1949), Piet Kramer (1881–1961), Michel De Klerk (1884–1923); **De Dageraad** (**E** F4).
Contemporary architecture
(Post-)modernism: functionalist, austere or experimental.
Beleefbibliotheek (**F** A1)
→ *Oosterdokskade 143*
Jo Coenen's giant library (2007);
Oostelijk Havengebied (**F** C1-F3)
Eastern dock district.

CITY PROFILE

- Capital of Holland
- 765 000 inhabitants
- 177 nationalities
- 600,000 bicycles
- Nine clock towers
- 165 canals
- 51 museums
- 6,800 listed buildings
- 11 million visitors/year

GETTING AROUND

Brug: bridge; **Dijk:** dike; **Gracht:** canal; **Huis:** house; **Kade:** quay; **Kerk:** church; **Markt:** market; **Plein:** square; **Stad:** town; **Steeg:** lane; **Straat:** street; **Toren:** tower

CANAL ON THE JORDAAN (BROUWERSGRACHT)

KEY DATES

13th–14th c. A fishing village on the River Amstel becomes a city. **15th–16th c.** Integration into the empire of Charles V. In 1578, the Protestants triumph over Catholic Spain. **17th c.** The 'Golden Age', an era of economic and artistic glory. The West & East Indies Companies consolidate themselves in Asia, Africa and the Americas. **19th c.** 1808: capital of the kingdom of Holland. Industrial Revolution. **20th c.** The Provo anarchist movement (active 1965–70) will gain a strong following.

WWW.

→ *iamsterdam.com*
The Tourist Office website.
→ *amsterdam.info*
→ *simplyamsterdam.nl*
Practical information, hotel reservations, etc.

Cybercafés
Beleefbibliotheek (F A1)
→ *Oosterdokskade 143*
Daily 10am–10pm
Free Internet.

Wi-Fi
Widespread in hotels, cafés, etc, and often free.

TOURIST INFO

ATCB (or VVV)
Tel. 0900 400 4040 (on site)
201 88 00 (from abroad)
Mon-Fri 9am–5pm
→ *Stationsplein (Mon-Fri 9am–6pm); Centraal Station (Tue-Sat 11am–7pm); Leidseplein 1 (Daily 9.30am–5.30pm in April-Sep)*
The Amsterdam Tourist Office (ATCB) outlets.

TELEPHONE

Telephone codes
Calling Amsterdam
→ *011 (from the USA) / 00 (from Europe)+ 31 (Holland) + 20 (Amsterdam and region) + seven-digit number*
Holland to the US/ UK
→ *00 + 1 (USA) / 44 (UK) + number*
Within Holland
→ *020 (except when in Amsterdam and its region) + number*
Special numbers
→ *They start with 0800 and 0900; no need to dial a code before; these numbers cannot be dialled from abroad*
Cell phones
→ *Beginning with 06; drop the 0 when calling from abroad*
Useful numbers
Police, fire service
→ *112*
Amsterdam Tourist Assistance Service (ATAS)
→ *Tel. 625 32 46*

DIARY OF EVENTS

Public holidays
→ *Jan 1; Good Friday, Easter Sun and Mon; April 30; May 5; Ascension Day; Whit Sun and Mon; Dec 25-26*
January
Amsterdam International Fashion Week
→ *Fourth week; amsterdamfashionweek.com*
Fashion festival: parades, parties in boutiques.
April-June
Museums Weekend
→ *Second or third weekend in April*
Free admission to national museums.
Koninginnedag
→ *April 30*
Street shows celebrate the Queen's birthday.
World Press Photo
→ *May-June, in Oude Kerk (**A** C3); worldpressphoto.org*
The world's biggest festival of photo-journalism. Exhibitions.

Liberation Day
→ *May 5, throughout the city*
Popular festival with street performances.
Art Amsterdam
→ *Five or six days mid-May, Amsterdam RAI, Europaplein (south of Pijp); artamsterdam.nl*
Modern and contemporary art fair.
Holland Festival
→ *The whole month, on several stages in town; hollandfestival.nl*
The country's biggest cultural event, with dance, movies, concerts, etc.
July
Festival on the IJ
→ *Ten days; overhetij.nl*
Dance, theater, music in the shipyards.
Openluchttheater
→ *All summer; openluchttheater.nl*
Open-air theater in the Vondelpark (**E** A1).
August
Gay Pride

Welcome to Amsterdam!

- **A** Centraal Station / Nieuwmarkt / Dam / Spui
- **B** Jordaan / Northern canals / Western islands
- **C** Southern canals / Leidseplein / Singel
- **D** Rembrandtplein / Amstel / Waterlooplein
- **E** Vondelpark / Museumplein / De Pijp
- **F** Plantage / Oosterdok / Zeeburg

Landmarks

- ANNE FRANK MUSEUM ★
- DAM ★
- BEGIJNHOF ★
- REMBRANDTPLEIN ★
- FLOWER MARKET ★
- GOLDEN CURVE ★
- RIJKSMUSEUM ★
- VAN GOGH MUSEUM ★
- CONCERTGEBOUW ★

Neighborhoods

- WESTERPARK
- JORDAAN
- OUDE STAD
- OUD-WEST
- ZUID
- DE PIJP

A

Centraal Station / Nieuwmarkt / Dam / Spui

The center of Amsterdam revolves around two main squares. To the west, the Dam, the historic heart from which the city derives its name, is surrounded by symbols of commercial glory (the Royal Palace, the Nieuwe Kerk and, further afield, the Stock Exchange). To the east, the Nieuwmarkt sports its dollhouse façades, unscathed by the passing of time. To the south, the Spui, the university neighborhood, draws intellectuals to its cafés, bookshops and book market. To the north lies the Red Light District: a maze of alleyways and crooked houses famous as the official area of prostitution, where a few fashion showrooms have recently started to make an appearance.

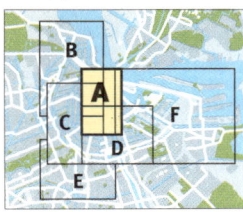

CAFÉ BERN

HEMELSE MODDER

RESTAURANTS

Vlaams
Frites Huis (**A** A5)
➜ *Voetboogstraat 33*
Daily 11am–6pm
The best 'Belgian' fries in town. €1.80–2.30.

Upstairs (**A** B5)
➜ *Grimburgwal 2*
Tel. 626 5603; Fri-Sun noon–6pm (5pm Sun)
On the upper story of a narrow building, the restaurant's 20 square yards only accommodate four tables. Sweet or savory pancakes from €6.

Kantjil en de Tijger (**A** A5)
➜ *Spuistraat 291-293*
Tel. 620 0994; Mon-Fri 4.30–11pm; Sat-Sun noon–11pm
At first sight, the Kantjil is hardly enticing, but it offers some of the city's best Indonesian cooking. Try the *nasi rames*, a combination of five Indonesian dishes, a simplified version of the gargantuan *rijsttafel* (€12–16.50). Dishes €8.

Harkema (**A** B4)
➜ *Nes 67; Tel. 428 2222*
Daily noon– 4pm, 5.30–10.30pm
Arty types and businessmen flock to this stylish contemporary brasserie designed by two local architects, Ronald Hooft and Herman Prast. With smooth, clean lines and plenty of space, prices here are no less attractive than the decor: excellent snacks. Dishes €14–18.

Café Bern (**A** D4)
➜ *Nieuwmarkt 9*
Tel. 622 0034; Daily 4pm–1am (service 6–11pm)
Highly prized for its cheese fondues. The ideal accompaniment is a steak, grilled at the table. Reserve. Fondue €14.50.

Kapitein Zeppo's (**A** B5)
➜ *Gebed Zonder End 5*
Tel. 624 2057; Daily noon–1am (2am Fri-Sat)
A quiet restaurant, tucked away at the end of an alley, mainly patronized by students and lecturers from the nearby university. Inventive, varied cooking (fried mussels, aubergine lasagne). Tables under the glass roof or outside. Prix fixe €34.50; dishes €19.

Hemelse Modder (**A** D3)
➜ *Oude Waal 11; Tel. 624 32 03; Tue-Sun 6–10pm*
Inviting menu (rainbow trout fillet with catfish and dill mousse) with a few vegetarian options (wild-mushroom pudding). The star turn is the chocolate mousse (or 'divine mud') that gives the place its name. Prix fixe €29.50; dishes €25.

EENHOUSE

CONSCIOUS DREAMS KOKOPELLI

DE HOED VAN TIJN

CAFÉS, COFFEESHOP

De Jaren (**A** B5)
→ *Nieuwe Doelenstraat 20*
Tel. 625 5771; Daily 10am–1am (2am Fri-Sat)
Unquestionably the most beautiful of all the city's 'big cafés', located in a former bank building. Sit inside, or on one of the two terraces overlooking the Amstel. Delicious sandwiches and salads.

De Drie Fleschjes (**A** B3)
→ *Gravenstraat 18*
Tel. 624 8443; Mon-Sat 2–8.30pm; Sun 3–8pm
An ancestral *proeflokaal* (1650). You drink standing up, between the counter and a row of old barrels replete with gin, brandy, liquors, beers and wines.

Greenhouse (**A** B4)
→ *Oudezijds Voorburgwal 191; Tel. 624 49 74*
Daily 9am–1am
The flagship of the Greenhouse chain of coffeeshops, whose reputation has increased since 1993 after winning the prestigious High Times and Cannabis cups.

THEATERS, CLUBS

Nes Theaters (**A** B4)
→ *Performances 8.30pm*
Three theaters, in a street that has been devoted to spectacle ever since the 19th century: comedies, dance, music-hall, mime.

Brakke grond
→ *Nes 45; Tel. 622 90 14*
A dynamic Flemish cultural center; pleasant bar.

Frascati
→ *Nes 63; Tel. 626 68 66*
Named after the Italian café that originally stood on this site.

De Engelenbak
→ *Nes 71; Tel. 626 36 44*
This major amateur theater venue has kick-started many a professional career. On Tuesday nights hopefuls flock to the 'Open Bak', or open stage.

Café Casablanca (**A** D2)
→ *Zeedijk 26*
Tel. 06 122 00 519 (cell phone); Daily 8pm–3am (4am Fri-Sat)
One of the oldest jazz clubs in the country (1946), it has has played host to countless stars, including the legendary saxophonist Kid Dynamite. Every week: concerts, karaoke and dancing (Wed-Sat).

Winston Kingdom (**A** C3)
→ *Warmoesstraat 131*
Tel. 623 13 80; Opening hours vary; winston.nl
Originally one of the bars of the Winston Hotel, it was turned into a nightclub with an eclectic musical program, launching many young Dutch groups in the process. The dance floor is invariably packed, with live music or DJs working in a wide range of styles.

De Buurvrouw (**A** B4)
→ *Sint Pieterspoortsteeg 29*
Tel. 625 9654; Daily 9pm–3am (4am Fri-Sat)
The favorite spot for inveterate nightowls after other clubs have closed for the night. Free entry.

SHOPPING

Het Grote Avontuur (**A** B1)
→ *Haarlemmerstraat 25*
Tel. 626 85 97
Daily 11am–6pm
Swedish clogs, Russian samovars, Indian prints: an array of objects from all over the world mingles with traditional Dutch motifs adorning fabrics and furniture.

Conscious Dreams Kokopelli (**A** C2)
→ *Warmoesstraat 12*
Tel. 421 7000
Daily 11am–10pm
This store sells Guarana capsules, magic mushrooms, books on ecstasy... The shop assistants are expert on the subjects and full of good advice. Internet café.

Jacob Hooy & Co (**A** C4)
→ *Kloveniersburgwal 12*
Tel. 624 3041
Mon 1–6pm; Tue-Sat 10am–6pm (5pm Sat)
A herbalist's shop, dating from 1743, with weathered barrels, cosmetic oils and drawers stuffed with teas, spices and medicinal herbs.

De Hoed van Tijn (**A** C4)
→ *Nieuwe Hoogstraat 15*
Tel. 623 2759; Mon noon–6pm; Tue-Sat 11am–6pm; Sun noon–5pm (Oct-Dec)
Hundreds of hats for men and women, from the classic Stetson to designer creations, some made to measure.

Supermarkt Oriental Commodities (**A** C4)
→ *Nieuwmarkt 27*
Tel. 626 27 97; Mon-Sat 9am–7pm (6pm Sat)
A well-stocked supermarket with products from various parts of Asia: Indonesian crackers, lotus seeds, makisu (mats for rolling sushi), etc.

De Stoelenwinkel (**A** D4)
→ *Oudeschans 40*
Tel. 693 54 52
Tue-Sat 10am (11am Sat)–5pm
Dozens of chairs, stools, and armchairs which have been reclaimed and recycled with stylish results.

Jordaan / Northern canals / Western islands

B

The relics of Jordaan's humble past can be seen in its modest houses bedecked with flowers and its convivial cafés. This zest for life has taken over the large canals and their side streets, now crammed with restaurants and colorful store displays. To the north, the docks of Prinseneiland, now lying idle, recall the city's seafaring past, while its old industrial buildings have been turned into arts venues: the old Westergasfabriek gasworks, a product of the Amsterdam School set in a working-class neighborhood, now serve as a cultural complex, while the NDSM art center lies beyond the sand bar of the IJ, on a dock in the throes of radical transformation.

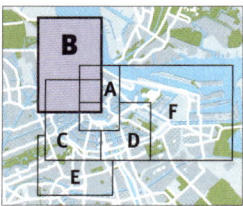

IJ-KANTINE

DE BOLHOED

RESTAURANTS

Small World (**B** C3)
➔ *Binnen Oranjestraat 14*
Tue-Sat 10.30am–8pm;
Sun noon–8pm
A tiny shop with a wide range of sandwiches, muffins, soups and fresh vegetable and fruit juices, to have in or take out. Good-natured Australian owner. Snacks €7.

Yam Yam (**B** A5)
➔ *Frederik Hendrik Straat 90; Tue-Sun 6–10pm*
Excellent pizzeria; try the house specialty: the pizza with truffles. €7.50–13.50.

IJ-Kantine (off **B** C1)
➔ *NDSM-Werf Ondinaweg 15-17; Tel. 633 7162*
Daily 9am–10pm
Close to the ferry terminal, this refurbished warehouse provides a cozy stop-off for visitors on their way to the northern docks. Food is served at the water's edge, or behind the bay windows overlooking the IJ. Dishes €13–19.

De Bolhoed (**B** C5)
➔ *Prinsengracht 60-62*
Tel. 626 1803
Daily noon (11am Sat)–10pm
For fans of vegetarian dishes. In the day: soups, quiches and sandwiches; in the evening: vegetables served with salad and brown rice. Homemade pies and cakes. Prix fixe €22; dishes €14.

De Belhamel (**B** D4)
➔ *Brouwersgracht 60*
Tel. 622 1095
Daily noon–4pm, 6–10pm
The gold-and-brown Art Deco interior alone warrants a visit. Very good seasonal cuisine, and the stunning views over Brouwersgracht and Herengracht. Popular, so reserve. Prix fixe €35–40; dishes €25.

La Salle du Jour (**B** C5)
➔ *Prinsenstraat 10*
Tel. 428 2455; Tue-Sun 6–10pm (10.30pm Thu-Sat)
Excellent fish restaurant with a Mediterranean slant, and a good choice of vegetarian dishes too. Beautiful black-and-white decor. Prix fixe €37–45.

CAFÉS, COFFEESHOP

De Blaffende Vis (**B** B4)
➔ *Westerstraat 118; Tel. 625 1721; Mon-Fri 10.30am–1am (3am Fri); Sat 9am–3am; Sun 9.30am–1am*
The light pours into this cheerful brown café, where regulars of all ages sip their beer on a high stool or on the mezzanine. Good food too, with such hearty dishes as sauerkraut and fish pie in

BARNEY'S

MOOOI

KITSCH KITCHEN SUPERMERCADO

the evening.
De Reiger (**B** B5)
→ *Nieuwe Leliestraat 34*
Tel. 624 7426; Mon-Fri
5pm–midnight (1am Wed-Fri); Sat 3pm–1am;
Sun 5pm–midnight
A wonderfully atmospheric old brown café, with century-old fittings, parquet floor and red velvet drapes. There's a small dining room at the back, often packed, serving excellent food.

Café Tabac (**B** C4)
→ *Brouwersgracht 101*
Tel. 622 4413; Tue-Fri 4pm–1am (3am Fri); Sat-Mon 11am–1am (3am Sat)
Laid-back setting on the edge of a canal and a young crowd, who spills outside on nice days. Opposite is the tiny brown café Het Papeneiland, dating from 1641.

Barney's (**B** D4)
→ *Haarlemmerstraat 102*
Tel. 625 9761; Daily 7am–1am (3am Fri-Sat)
Another prize-winning coffeeshop, now an institution. See also Barney's Farm, at no. 98.

BAR, CLUB

Café Nol (**B** B4)
→ *Westerstraat 109*
Tel. 624 5380; Daily 9pm–3am (4am Fri-Sat)
This café bathed in red light, with live singers and a soundtrack of golden oldies, beautifully recaptures the spirit of Jordaan's former cabarets.

Bitterzoet (**B** D5)
→ *Spuistraat 2*
Tel. 421 2318; Opening hours vary; bitterzoet.nl
One of the best clubs in the city, with live bands followed by DJs spinning soul, hip-hop and reggae, and occasionally rock or salsa. Laid-back atmosphere and no dress code.

SAUNA

Sauna Deco (**B** C5)
→ *Herengracht 115*
Tel. 623 8215; Mon-Sat noon (3pm Sat)–11pm; Sun 1–7pm
The fine paneling, stained glass and ornate bronze balustrades in this 1920s Art Deco sauna were salvaged from the Bon Marché department store in Paris, when the shop interior was remodeled. Turkish baths, massages, reflexology treatments. Note: the sauna is mixed.

CULTURAL CENTER, CINEMA

Westergasfabriek (**B** A3)
→ *Haarlemmerweg 8-10*
Tel. 586 0710
westergasfabriek.nl
An old gas factory converted into a huge, fascinating cultural complex with a theater, movie theater, festivals, exhibitions. Check their program on the website.

The Movies (**B** C3)
→ *Haarlemmerdijk 161*
Tel. 638 6016
A lovely early 20th-century movie theater, with an Art Deco interior and café-restaurant.

SHOPPING

House of Tattoos (**B** C3)
→ *Haarlemmerdijk 130c*
Tel. 330 9046; By appt: Mon-Sat 11am–6pm; Sun 1–6pm
Tattoos after consultation with Sjab Horwitz, who will help you create your own design. For over-18s and by appointment only.

Moooi (**B** B4)
→ *Westerstraat 187; Tel. 528 7760; Tue-Sat 10am–6pm (9pm Thu); Sun noon–6pm*
A gallery-store selling designer furniture – armchairs, tables, couches, decorative objects – in a modern streamlined or consciously retro style, dramatically displayed against a bright white background.

Kitsch Kitchen Supermercado (**B** B6)
→ *Rozengracht 8-12*
Tel. 622 8261; Mon-Sat 10am–6pm; Sun noon–5pm
Useful and decorative gifts for the home, with some great ideas for children too, all in a wide range of bright colors.

Brilmuseum Brillenwinkel (**B** C6)
→ *Gasthuismolensteeg 7*
Tel. 421 2414; Wed-Sat 11am–5.30pm (5pm Sat)
A small spectacle museum-cum-store with hundreds of different types of spectacles, dating from the 19th century to the present day.

Vezjun (**B** B6)
→ *Rozengracht 110*
Tue-Fri noon–7pm (8pm Thu); Sat 11am–6pm
A fashion boutique devoted to Dutch designers – a rarity in Amsterdam.

SPRMRKT (**B** A6)
→ *Rozengracht 191-193*
Tel. 330 5601; Daily 10am (noon Sun-Mon)–6pm (8pm Thu)
A trendy underground hideout dedicated to the 1970s, with period furniture, clothes, light fittings, and pieces of art. Another store at: *Nieuwezijds Voorburgwal 262* (**B** C6).

The three main powers of the Golden Age are evoked in canals that boast the city's most imposing façades: the Herengracht ('of the Lords'), Keizersgracht ('of the Emperor') and Prinsengracht ('of the Prince'). Close by, café terraces and street musicians jostle for space on Leidseplein, where movie theaters and clubs stay open late, while the Leidsestraat and the area called the '9 Streets' (running from Reestraat to Wijde Heisteeg) are dotted with smart boutiques. Further south lies Nieuwe Spiegelstraat, the domain of antique dealers. To the northeast, the elegant Mint Tower surveys the tourists milling about in the flower market below.

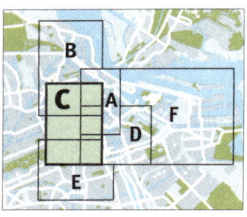

VAN DE KAART

DE SCHUTTER

RESTAURANTS

Buffet van Odette (**C** C2)
→ *Herengracht 309*
Tel. 423 6034; Mon, Wed-Fri 8.30am–4.30pm; Sat-Sun 10am–5.30pm
This tiny deli-café prepares organic salads, sandwiches, omelets and cakes, to take out or eat in, or at one of the tables outside. Snacks €5; dishes €10–15.

A la Plancha (**C** B3)
→ *1st Looiersdwarsstraat 15*
Tel. 420 3633
Tue-Sun 4pm–3am
Authentic tapas bar, with squid, seafood, Serrano ham and marinated olives, all prepared and served until closing time. Tapa €4.50; dishes €12–25.

Rose's Cantina (**C** D4)
→ *Reguliersdwarsstraat 38-40; Tel. 625 9797; Daily 5–10.30pm (11pm Fri-Sat)*
The menu here is based on classic Mexican recipes (enchiladas, guacamole, nachos) and changes regularly. Cocktail bar open every night until 2am. Dishes €20.

Van de Kaart (**C** B4)
→ *Prinsengracht 512*
Tel. 625 9232
Mon-Sat 6–10.30pm
The atmosphere in this starkly decorated mezzanine grows increasingly animated as the night goes on. Elaborate cooking (confit of rabbit pâté with pistachios, roast fillet of venison with a terrine of puréed green cabbage and bacon) and erudite wine list. Prix fixe €34.50; dishes €20.50.

Garlic Queen (**C** C4)
→ *Reguliersdwarsstraat 27*
Tel. 422 6426
Wed-Sun 5–10pm
The 55 lbs of bulbs ordered every week even end up in some unlikely main courses and desserts, but the result is subtle and very tasty. Try the gambas with chili and curried rice. Reserve. Prix fixe €32; dishes €25.

D'theeboom (**C** C1)
→ *Singel 210; Tel. 623 8420*
Mon-Sat 6–10pm
Subtle French recipes in an old cheese warehouse dating from 1712. Superb wine list. Prix fixe €35–40.

CAFÉS

Café Eijlders (**C** B4)
→ *Korte Leidsedwarsstraat 47; Tel. 624 2704*
Mon, Thu-Sun noon–1am (2am Fri-Sat); Tue-Wed 4pm–1am
An authentic brown café with dark wood trim and

BOURBONSTREET

THE FROZEN FOUNTAIN

KRAMER KUNST & ANTIEK

smoke-stained mirrors. Poetry readings every third Sunday of the month, as well as occasional exhibitions and live music.

De Schutter (**C** C3)
→ *Voetboogstraat 13-15 Tel. 622 4608; Daily noon–1am (3am Fri-Sat)*
Set in a historic 16th-century building, this brown café, a favorite haunt of students, also doubles as an informal restaurant. Wooden tables, candles and, for dessert, typical *poffertje* (tiny fluffy pancakes).

BARS, SHOWS

De Zotte (**C** B4)
→ *Raamstraat 29 Tel. 626 8694; Daily 4pm–1am (3am Fri-Sat)*
Off the beaten track, a small bar renowned for its selection of around 120 Belgian beers and for its generously sized dishes.

Whiskycafé L&B (**C** B5)
→ *Korte Leidsedwarsstraat 82-84; Tel. 625 2387; Daily 8pm–3am (4am Fri-Sat)*
Airy world or jazz music provides a wonderful backdrop for a glass of whisky. The walls are covered with bottles, indicating the staggering choice available, with further details posted on large signboards.

Alto Jazz Café (**C** B4)
→ *Korte Leidsedwarsstraat 115; Tel. 626 3249; Daily 9pm–3am (4am Fri-Sat)*
Top-level jazz and salsa musicians revel in the chance to play to packed crowds in this intimate venue and, when the mood hits, get them dancing between the tables.

Bourbonstreet (**C** B4)
→ *Leidsekruisstraat 6-8 Tel. 623 3440; Daily 10pm–4am (5am Fri-Sat)*
This venue with parquet flooring, reminiscent of an old-style saloon, is dominated by a stage where talented musicians indulge in blues evenings and jam sessions. It fills up quickly after 11pm.

Boom Chicago (**C** B4)
→ *Leidseplein 12 Tel. 423 0101 (box office) Dinner: daily 6.30pm (6 & 8pm Sat); show: daily 8.15pm (7.30 & 10.30pm Sat)*
A very popular theater where comedies are staged in English. Dinner is also served before the performances.

Melkweg (**C** B4)
→ *Lijnbaansgracht 234a Tel. 531 8181 www.melkweg.nl*
A meeting point for hippies in the 1970s, it is now a versatile cultural center with exhibitions, concerts, movies and music evenings (electro, pop and 1980s).

Paradiso (**C** B5)
→ *Weteringschans 6-8 Tel. 626 4521 www.paradiso.nl*
A famous concert hall situated in a disused church, which promotes both local groups and international stars alike.

SHOPPING

Fifties-Sixties (**C** B2)
→ *Reestraat 5; Tel. 623 2653 Tue-Sat 1–6pm (5.30pm Sat)*
A clutter of ironware and household goods from the 1930s to the 1970s: ashtrays, lamps, toasters.

De Kaaskamer (**C** B3)
→ *Runstraat 7 Tel. 623 3483; Tue-Sat 9am–6pm (5pm Sat); Sun-Mon noon–5pm (6pm Mon)*
The best cheese shop in town sells a large selection of country cheeses, Goudas, *Friese Nagel* cheese (flavored with cloves) and *Leidse* cheese (with cumin).

The Frozen Fountain (**C** B3)
→ *Prinsengracht 645 Tel. 622 9375; Tue-Sat 10am–6pm; Sun 1–5pm*
This large hall displays the best of contemporary design.

Nieuwe Spiegelstraat (**C** C4-5)
The antique dealers' street.

Meulendijks & Schuil (**C** C4)
→ *No 45a; Tel. 620 0300 Mon-Sat 10am–6pm*
Telescopes, model ships, globes...

Kramer Kunst & Antiek (**C** C5)
→ *Corner of Prinsengracht Tel. 626 1116; Mon-Sat 11am–6pm; Sun 1–6pm*
Items from the 16th to early 20th centuries: Delft pottery, tiles and dolls.

Hester Van Eeghen (**C** B2)
→ *Hartenstraat 1 and 37 Tel. 626 9212; Mon 1–6pm; Tue-Sat 11am–6pm*
A hint of fantasy, a few spangles and warm shades of color feature on boots, shoes, slippers and bags by Hester Van Eeghen, a modern fashion designer.

Maranon Hammocks BV (**C** C3)
→ *Singel 488-490 Tel. 622 5938; Daily 10am–6pm (11am–5.30pm Oct-Feb)*
Hammocks and mosquito nets in all colors and sizes, suited both to home use and to taking on journeys.

Southern canals / Amstel / Rembrandtplein

Reguliersdwarsstraat and Amstelstraat, tucked away behind the river Amstel, boast the greatest number of gay nightclubs and meeting places in the city. These two streets open onto the Rembrandtplein, where other urban groups gather in more cafés and clubs. To the south, the pretty Reguliersgracht, and Utrechtsestraat, studded with restaurants, lead to the Amstelkerk church, with its peaceful square where children play hopscotch opposite the shaded terraces of the cafés. Moving northward, the Amstel leads to five synagogues surrounding Waterlooplein, vestiges of the old Jewish Quarter, now largely demolished.

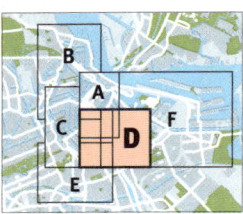

SOUP EN ZO

DE HUYSCHKAEMER

RESTAURANTS

Van Dobben (**D** B2)
→ *Korte Reguliersdwarsstraat 5; Tel. 624 4200*
Mon-Sat 9.30am–1am (2am Fri-Sat); Sun 11.30am–8pm
An institution in the city, this place is never empty. The specialty is *broodje*, soft rolls with a filling of your choice (tomato, sardine, ham, *kroket*, etc.) to take out or eat in. *Broodje* €2.50–5.

Soup en Zo (**D** C1)
→ *Jodenbreestraat 94*
Mon-Fri 11am–8pm;
Sat-Sun noon–7pm
Tasty seasonal soups to eat in or take out: spinach, coconut and coriander, tuscan bean etc. Also freshly-pressed juices. Another shop at *Nieuwe Spiegelstraat 54* (**C** C4). Soup €2.70–5.90.

Lo Stivale d'Oro (**D** C2)
→ *Amstelstraat 49; Tel. 638 7307; Wed-Mon 5–10.30pm*
This may look like a run-of-the-mill trattoria but the food is out of the ordinary. Farfalle with broccoli, tagliatelle with salmon or paprika, squid and pizzas. Pizza €9; dishes €14.

Tujuh Maret (**D** B3)
→ *Utrechtsestraat 73*
Tel. 427 9865
Daily noon–11pm
According to many this is the best Indonesian restaurant in Amsterdam. To try everything, choose an assortment of dishes: *nasi rames* (five plates), *nasi kuning Tujuh Maret* (ten plates), *rijsttafel Mina Hasa* (18 plates!)... served with rice, prawn crackers, and coleslaw. Sweet, spicy or very spicy on request. Annex at no. 65 (**D** B3), serving Tibetan specialties (*Thu-Sun 5–11pm*). Dishes €19–21.

Take Thaï (**D** B3)
→ *Utrechtsestraat 87*
Tel. 622 0577
Daily 6–10.30pm
A fashionable Thai restaurant with a minimalist white decor, where you dine by candlelight. Amongst their authentic, delicious dishes, the roast duck in soy sauce is worth trying. Prix fixe €29–40.50; dishes €19–22.

Van Vlanderen (**D** A4)
→ *Weteringschans 175*
Tel. 622 8292; Tue-Sat 6.30 (7pm Fri-Sat)–10.30pm
The superb French-Mediterranean (and Michelin-starred) cuisine of Marc Philippart includes such delights as truffled scallops, meltingly fresh cod, or veal steak with asparagus. Stylish

VAS OP DE 7DE   **PUCCINI BOMBONI**   **HET FORT VAN SJAKOO**

setting with outside space in summer; very friendly service. Reservations advised. Prix fixe €42–50.

CAFÉS

De Huyschkaemer (D C3)
➔ Utrechtsestraat 137
Tel. 627 0575; Daily 11.30am–1am (3am Fri-Sat)
This cozy, small, split-level café-restaurant with mosaic floors has indeed much of the atmosphere of a *huyschkammer*, or 'living room'. The clientele is mostly gay.

Brasserie Schiller (D B2)
➔ Rembrandtplein 26-36
Tel. 554 0700
Daily 3–10.30pm
The epitome of Art Deco, this traditional restaurant dates from 1912 (as does the Café Schiller next door). Eat on the terrace, or in the Portrait Room, surrounded by the 'Between Lunch and Dinner' series of paintings by Fritz Schiller, the businessman and part-time artist who imbued the place with the spirit that is still palpable today.

Café De Sluyswacht (D C1)
➔ Jodenbreestraat 1
Tel. 625 7611; Daily noon–1am (3am Fri-Sat; 7pm Sun)
Set in a narrow lock keeper's house that is now almost 300 years old, with a large terrace on the banks of the Oudeschans.

BARS, CLUBS, OPERA

Arc (D A2)
➔ Reguliersdwarsstraat 44
Tel. 689 7070; Daily 4pm–1am (Fri-Sat 3am)
One of the most fashionable cocktail bars on the street that has become the hub of Amsterdam's gay community. Various settings with smart decoration, light snacks and newspapers to read.

Mulligans (D B2)
➔ Amstel 100; Tel. 622 1330
Mon-Fri 4pm–1am (3am Fri); Sat-Sun 2pm–1am (3am Sat)
An Irish pub with live traditional Irish music (9.30pm Thu; 10pm Fri and Sat; open stage 7pm on Sun); also sometimes concerts (Wed) and traditional dance (Mon).

Canvas op de 7de (off D E4)
➔ Wibautstraat 150
Tel. 716 3817; Daily 11am–1am (3am Fri-Sat)
A hip, chic yet informal restaurant-club-art gallery on the seventh floor of an old press bureau. Good food and good music (soul on Thu, techno and house on Fri-Sat).

Escape (D B2)
➔ Rembrandtplein 11
Tel. 622 1111; Thu-Sun 11pm–4am (5am Fri-Sat)
The most popular house and techno club in the city; local and international stars stand at the turntables

Het Muziektheater (D C1)
➔ Waterlooplein 22; Tel. 551 8117; hetmuziektheater.nl
The home of the National Ballet and the Nederlandse Opera is part of the Stopera complex, built in 1986 by Cees Dam and Wilhelm Holzbauer, and also contains the town hall. Front-rank companies and musicians from all over the world come here to perform.

SHOPPING

Concerto (D B3)
➔ Utrechtsestraat 52-60
Tel. 623 5228
Mon-Sat 10am–6pm (9pm Thu); Sun noon–6pm
CDs and vinyl covering a host of musical styles (classical, jazz, reggae, funk, etc.). A few rare treasures.

Puccini Bomboni (D B1)
➔ Staalstraat 17 (D B1)
Tel. 626 5474; Daily 9am (noon Sun-Mon)–6pm
➔ Singel 184 (C C1); Daily 11am (noon Sun-Mon)–6pm
Passersby swoon over the window here, looking at what may be some of the best pralines and chocolates in town.

Droog Design (D B1)
➔ Staalstraat 7b
Tel. 523 50 59; Tue-Sat 11am–6pm; Sun noon–5pm
One of the most fashionable designer names in Holland, selling everyday items, furniture, works of art and many other original creations.

Waterloopleinmarkt (D C1)
➔ Waterlooplein; Mon-Sat 9am–5pm (variable)
The biggest and oldest of the city's flea markets where you can find everything: Indonesian fabrics, African crafts, second-hand clothes, shoes, and much more.

Het Fort van Sjakoo (D C1)
➔ Jodenbreestraat 24
Tel. 625 8979; Mon-Sat 11am–6pm (5pm Sat)
An extraordinary political bookstore, where you can flick through a vast range of books, from the adventures of a punk Tintin to a pirate radio manual or an ABC of squatters' rights.

Vondelpark / Museumplein / De Pijp

To the south of Stadhouderskade lies the prestigious museum district. Luxury stores and haute couture designers hold court on P.C. Hoofstraat and Van Baerlestraat, while the private hotels and middle-class houses around Vondelpark enjoy an enviable calm. Southeast, in contrast, the Pijp, a multicultural and student district teems with exotic restaurants and inviting cafés. Further on, the Plan zuid (South Plan) is a city planning project drawn up by Berlage and enriched by the architects of the Amsterdam School, as in the case of the workers' residential complex of De Dageraad.

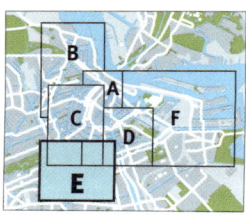

BAZAR

CONTRAST

RESTAURANTS

Siempre Tapas (E E2)
→ *1st Sweelinckstraat 23*
Tel. 671 8616
Daily 4pm–midnight
An ideal stop after a tour of the Sarphatipark or Albert Cuypmarkt. This quaint café decorated with white and blue tiles serves a large selection of genuinely good tapas and other Spanish dishes. Sit near the fireplace or, in summer, on the terrace. Tapa, dishes €5–11.

Bazar (E E2)
→ *Albert Cuypstraat 182*
Tel. 675 0544; Mon-Fri 11am–1am (2am Fri); Sat 9am–2am; Sun 9am–midnight
This former synagogue opening onto the Albert Cuypmarkt is now a restaurant offering Middle Eastern delicacies: kebabs, falafels, couscous and yoghurt with honey. Dishes €12.

De Ondeugd (E D2)
→ *Ferdinand Bolstraat 13*
Tel. 672 0651; Daily 6–11pm
Elaborate cooking but, above all, an interior worthy of a nightclub: luminous motifs on the walls, mirror balls on the ceiling, chandeliers fitted with strange light bulbs, etc. The menu is an inspired marriage of tradition and fantasy, French and Italian influences: carpaccio with parmesan and pine nuts, parsnip soup, mussels in two types of sauce. Dishes €18.

Contrast (E D3)
→ *Ferdinand Bolstraat 176-178; Tel. 471 5544*
Tue-Sun noon–1am (2am Fri-Sat; midnight Sun)
Both the dining room and the wine bar are smart and intimate, with striking black-and-white contrasts in the decor. The Franco-Dutch menu recommends a specific wine for each dish. Very pleasant terrace in summer. Dishes €23.

Stof (E E3)
→ *Van der Helstplein 9*
Tel. 364 0354; Daily 6–10pm
A cozy café-restaurant in a lovely square where the tables are adorned with candles (and bouquets of tulips in April). Inventive seasonal cooking: chicken marinated in mustard and brandy, lamb in honey and thyme sauce, zander fillet with shrimps. Convivial and welcoming. Prix fixe €26.

Pulpo (E A2)
→ *Willemsparkweg 87*
Tel. 676 0700; Mon-Sat noon–3pm, 5.30–10pm
A varied menu of meat, fish and vegetarian

AART VAN M'N TANTE

DE BADCUYP

BETSY PALMER

dishes, all with a strong Mediterranean influence, is served in an elegant minimalist setting. Reservation advised. Prix fixe €29.

PÂTISSERIES

De Taart van m'n Tante (**E** D3)
→ Ferdinand Bolstraat 10
Tel. 776 4600
Daily 10am–6pm
A kitsch and eccentric patisserie, tearoom and B&B rolled into one, with vividly colorful decor. The variety of cakes is huge.
Bakkerswinkel (**E** C3)
→ Roelof Hartstraat 68
Tel. 662 3594
Tue-Sat 7am–6pm (5pm Sat); Sun 10am–4pm
A different, but equally popular, bakery and tearoom, renowned for the quality and freshness of its products. Extensive snack menu.

CAFÉS, BARS, COFFEESHOP

Vertigo (**E** A1)
→ Vondelpark 3; Tel. 612 3021; Daily 10am–1am
The terrace of the bar-restaurant Vertigo, at the foot of the Filmmuseum, is arguably one of the most beautiful in Amsterdam and offers wonderful views of the Vondelpark. Excellent choice of beers.
Cobra (**E** C2)
→ Hobbemastraat 18
Tel. 470 0111; Daily 10am–6pm (8pm in summer)
In summer this spacious steel-and-glass café puts around 200 chairs out on Museum plein. The interior is the realm of artists from the CoBrA movement.
Goene Vindler (**E** E2)
→ Albert Cuypstraat 130
Tel. 470 2500; Daily 10am–1am (3am Fri-Sat)
A very pleasant brown café in the heart of the market. Food in the evening.
Yo-Yo (**E** F2)
→ 2e Jan van der Heijdenstraat 79; Tel. 664 7173; Mon-Sat noon–7pm
A much quieter coffeeshop than in the center. 'Organic' herb.
Blauwe Theehuis (**E** A2)
→ Vondelpark 5; Tel. 662 0254; June-Oct: daily 9am–1am (3am Fri-Sat); Nov-May: daily 9am–6pm (11pm Thu-Sun; 1am Fri-Sat)
A slightly shabby flying saucer sits in the middle of the Vondelpark! Warm and cozy in winter, and with a gorgeous terrace in summer; jazz concerts on Sunday afternoons and DJs on Friday nights.
De Badcuyp (**E** E2)
→ 1e Sweelinckstraat 10
Tel. 675 96 69; Tue-Sun 11am–1am (Fri-Sat 3am)
The owner of this bar was once a jazz musician and his live program leans heavily on jazz, although it also features world music and soul. The concerts on the ground floor feature established names, while the more intimate loft setting showcases emerging talents.

CINEMA

Rialto (**E** E3)
→ Ceintuurbaan 338
Tel. 662 3488
www.rialtofilm.nl
The Rialto was built to replace a neighborhood movie theater that opened in 1928, and is as friendly as its predecessor. Art house films; several bars.

SHOPPING

Azzuro Due (**E** B1)
→ Pietre Cornelisz Hooftstraat 138; Tel. 671 9708; Mon 1–6pm; Tue-Sat 10am–6pm; Sun noon–5pm
This trail-blazing shop in a street devoted to fashion sell ready-to-wear clothes, shoes, bags and other accessories from a select range of designer labels.
Betsy Palmer (**E** F3)
→ Van Woustraat 46
Tel. 470 9795; Mon-Sat 10am (noon Mon)–6pm (5pm Sat)
A smartly designed store selling fashionable women's shoes in unusual colors. Another shop at Rokin 9-15 (**A** B4).
Duikelman (**E** D2)
→ Ferdinand Bolstraat 68
Tel. 671 2230; Tue-Sat 9.30am–6pm (5pm Sat)
A gold mine for keen cooks, it stocks over 10,000 items, from citrus presses to skillets, spatulas to cookbooks. Another shop at Gerard Doustraat 54 (**E** E2).
De Kinderfeestwinkel (**E** E2)
→ Gerard Doustraat 65-67
Tel. 672 2215
Daily 10am–6pm
A magical toyshop, guaranteed to thrill every child, and probably adults as well.
Jambe (**E** E3)
→ Van der Helstplein 6
Tel. 664 4227; Tue-Sat 9am–4pm (3pm Sat)
This small shop was founded as an outlet for goods produced by members of an association of disabled people fresh from training courses. Craft items and tidbits.

Plantage / Oosterdok / Zeeburg

The Plantage, a middle-class neighborhood studded with gardens, is home to the city zoo, a botanical garden and, to the south, a thrilling Tropical Museum. To the north, beyond the Entrepotdok, a harbor lined with superbly restored warehouses, the historic port is now in the midst of redevelopment but still offers pleasant strolls. To the east of the cutting-edge ARCAM cultural center, the peninsulas of Zeeburg have become open-air museums of contemporary architecture, intent on supplying their inhabitants with ideal living conditions. The docks are no longer operational but are gradually starting to play host to nighttime leisure activities.

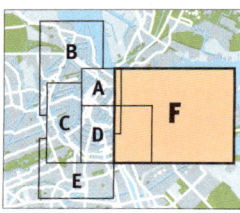

KOFFIEHUIS V. D. VOLKSBOND

BROUWERIJ'T IJ

RESTAURANTS

Frank's Smoke House (F C2)
→ *Wittenburgergracht 303*
Tel. 670 0774; Mon-Sat 9am–6pm (4pm Mon; 5pm Sat)
Frank sells his own freshly cured salmon, but also every type of meat. These mouthwatering delicacies can be eaten either by the plate or wrapped up in a sandwich. Dishes €15–17.

Kilimanjaro (F A2)
→ *Rapenburgerplein 6*
Tel. 622 3485
Tue-Sun 5–10pm
The menu of this friendly restaurant offers a crash tour of African cuisine, with an emphasis on specialties from Ethiopia and its neighbor, Eritrea. African wines, beers and cocktails. Dishes €16.

Koffiehuis van den Volksbond (F B2)
→ *Kadijksplein 4*
Tel. 622 1209; Daily 6–10pm
At the north end of Entrepotdok, the erstwhile 'coffee house' for dockers is now a popular restaurant, with huge meals at incredibly good prices. Dishes €16.

Teatro (F B2)
→ *Kadijksplein 16; Tel. 623 6313; Mon-Sat 6–10pm*
No pizzas here but duck ravioli, bream cooked in sea salt, carpaccios, risottos, to be eaten in a candlelit dining room. Dishes €25.

Greetje (F A2)
→ *Peperstraat 23*
Tel. 779 7450; Tue-Sat 6–10pm (11pm Fri-Sat)
Inspired by the recipes of his mother Greetje, René Loven breathes new life into traditional Dutch cuisine. His inventive cooking is grounded in local ingredients: duck terrine on toast, blood sausage with warm apples, spiced-bread mousse. Warm, suitably old-fashioned setting. Dishes €25.

CAFÉS

Amstelhaven (F A4)
→ *Mauritskade 1; Tel. 665 2672; Daily 11am–1am (6pm Mon-Tue; 3am Fri-Sat)*
This café's location, under a road by the water's edge, may be unpromising but its modern, white décor and terrace on the canal attracts a young, sophisticated crowd. DJ sessions at the weekend.

Eik en Linde (F B3)
→ *Plantage Middenlaan 22 Tel. 622 5716; Mon-Sat 11am–1am (2am Fri-Sat)*
A neighborhood favorite, this is a highly enjoyable,

MUZIEKGEBOUW AAN HET IJ

PAKHUIS DE ZWIJGER

archetypal Dutch brown bar dating from 1858. The place really starts to fill up in the early evening.

De Druif (F A2)
→ Rapenburgerplein 83
Tel. 624 4530; Mon, Wed-Sun 4pm–1am (3am Fri-Sat)
'The Grape' is a genuine brown café in the old port neighborhood, with the obligatory coating of nicotine on the walls.

Brouwerij't IJ (F C3)
→ Funenkade 7; Tel. 622 8325; Daily 3–8pm
This café, located in a windmill, brews its own beer. Mostly locals pack this narrow place, standing (there are no tables) and drinking around the bar.

BARS, CLUBS

De Kluis (F B2)
→ Prins Hendrikkade 194
Tel. 420 2282; Daily 10am–1am (3am Fri-Sat)
A Brazilian bar and dance hall where a cosmopolitan clientele strut their stuff with abandon to the sounds of live Latin bands.

Café Pakhuis Wilhelmina (F D1)
→ Veemkade 576
Tel. 419 3368
cafepakhuiswilhelmina.nl
This old warehouse facing Java-eiland was occupied by squatters back in 1988, and now provides a stage for aspiring local musicians. Its eclectic program embraces rock, folk, soul and samba, as well as allowing students from the Conservatory to premiere their compositions. The hard rock karaoke is famous.

Restaurant-club Panama (F D2)
→ Oostelijke Handelskade 4
Tel. 311 8686; Restaurant: daily noon–11pm; shows Thu-Sun nights
This nightclub in a former port authority building attracts diehard party people and caters to a wide range of tastes: funk and electro nights, rock and jazz concerts (last Sun of the month). Restaurant with hip industrial touches in its decoration.

THEATER, CONCERTS

Tropentheater (F C4)
→ Mauritskade 63 & Linnaeusstraat 2
Tel. 568 8711
An extensive cultural program about non-Western countries. Latino-American and African dance, plays, lectures, movies and conferences all year round.

Bimhuis (F B1)
→ Piet Heinkade 3; Tel. 788 2150; www.bimhuis.nl
Adjacent to the previous building, Amsterdam's most important jazz venue plays host to top musicians from around the world.

Muziekgebouw aan het IJ (F B1)
→ Piet Heinkade 1; Tel. 788 2010; Café Star Ferry: daily 10am–11pm
This state-of-the-art concert hall (2005) offers impeccable acoustics for classical, contemporary and world music. The auditorium and foyer seat 725 and 100, respectively, while the panoramic café (Star Ferry) overlooks the boats passing to and fro.

CINEMA, CULTURAL CENTERS

Studio K (F D3)
→ Timorplein 62
Tel. 692 0422; Café: daily 11am–1am (3am Fri-Sat)
This art house movie theater sometimes doubles as a club at the weekend. Films from all over the world and a quirky café with deliberately mismatched antique furniture and a terrace on the square in summer.

ARCAM (F B2)
→ Prins Hendrikkade 600
Tel. 620 4878; Tue-Sat 1–5pm
The museum of the ARCAM architectural foundation occupies the top floor of an impressive curved building designed in 2003 by René Van Zuuk. Exhibitions, magazines, maps offering various tours of the city, all on the subject of architecture.

Pakhuis De Zwijger (F C1)
→ Piet Heinkade 179
Tel. 788 4440; Café: Mon-Fri 9am–11pm (midnight Fri)
Readings, documentaries, workshops: stimulating ideas are the order of the day in this warehouse converted into a cultural laboratory. Concerts, exhibitions and café-gallery set between two expanses of water.

SHOPPING

Pol's Potten (F E1)
→ KNSM Laan 39; Tel. 419 3541; Sun noon–5pm; Mon-Sat 10am (noon Mon)–6pm
The household objects displayed seemingly at random in this huge emporium include wonderful bargains: furniture, lamps, crockery and pottery, in styles ranging from the quaintly old-fashioned to the sleekly modern.

Transportation and hotels in Amsterdam

Street names, monuments and places to visit are listed alphabetically. They are followed by a map reference of which the initial letter in bold (**A**, **B**, **C**...) relates to the district and matching map.

Streets

'S Graven-Hekje **F** A2
'S Gravelandseveer
  A B5-C5, **D** B1
1e Bloemdwarsstraat
  B B5
1e Constantijn Huygensstr.
  C A5-A6, **E** A1-B1
1e Jan Steenstr. **E** D3-E3
1e Jan Van Der
  Heijdenstraat **E** D3-E3
1e Looiersdwarsstraat
  C B3
1e Nassaustraat **B** A3-B3
1e Rozendwarsstr.
  C A1-B2, **B** B6
1e Sweelinckstraat **E** E2
1e Van D. Helststr. **E** E2-E3
1e Weteringdwarsstraat
  C C5, **E** D1
1e Weteringplantsoen
  E D1-D2
2e Bloemdwarsstraat
  B B5-B6, **C** A1
2e Egelantdw. str. **B** B5
2e Jacob Van
  Campenstraat **E** E2
2e Jan Van Der
  Heijdenstraat **E** F2-F3
2e Laurierdwarsstr. **C** A2
2e Leliedwarsstraat **B** B5
2e Looiersdwarsstraat
  C A3
2e Nassaustraat **B** A3-B3
2e Rozendwarsstraat
  B B5-B6, **C** A2
2e Tuindw. str. **B** B5
2e Van der Helststr. **E** E4
2e Weteringdwarsstraat
  C C5, **E** D1
2e Weteringplantsoen
  D A4
3e Weteringdwarsstraat
  C C5, **E** D1
Anne Frankstraat **F** A2
Achterburgwal **A** B4-C4
Achtergracht **D** C3, **E** F1
Achter Oosteinde **D** C4

Albert Cuypstraat **E** D3-F2
Alexander Boersstr. **E** B2
Alexanderkade **F** C3
Alexanderplein **F** C3-C4
Alexanderstraat **F** C3
Amstel **A** B6-C6, **D** C1-D3
Amsteldijk **D** E4
Amstelkade **E** C4-F4
Amstelstr. **A** C6, **D** B2-C2
Amstelveld **D** B3, **E** E1
Apollolaan **E** C4
Assendelftstraat **B** B2
Azartplein **F** E1
Baanburgsteeg **B** C3
Bachplein **E** B4
Bakkersstraat **D** B2
Balthasar Floriszstr. **E** C3
Banstraat **E** A2-A3
Barentszplein **B** C2
Barentszstraat **B** C2
Barndesteeg **A** C4
Beethovenstraat **E** B4
Berenstraat **C** B2
Beursplein **A** B3, **B** D5-D6
Beursstraat **A** B3-C3,
  B D5
Bickersgracht **B** C2-C3
Binnen Bantammerstraat
  A D3
Binnen Oranjestraat **B** C3
Binnen Wieringerstr.
  B D4
Binnengasthuisstraat
  A B5, **D** B1
Binnenkant **A** D3, **F** B1
Blauwbrug
  A C6-D6, **D** C2
Blauwburgwal **A** A2, **B** C5
Bloedstraat **A** C3
Bloemstraat **B** A6-B5,
  C A1-B1
Breitnerstraat **E** A3-A4
Bronckhorststraat **E** B3
Brouwersgracht **B** B3-D4
Brouwersstraat **A** A1,
  B C4-D4
Buiten **B** C3
Ceintuurbaan **E** D3-F3

Concertgebouwplein
  E B2
Cornelis Anthoniszstraat
  E C3
Cornelis Schuystr. **E** A2-A3
Cornelis Troostplein
  E C4-D4
Cruquiuskade **F** C3-D3
Dam **A** B3, **B** D6
Damrak **A** B3-C2, **B** D5-D6
Damstraat **A** B4, **B** D6
Daniël Stalpertstr. **E** D2
Dapperplein **F** D4
Dapperstraat **F** C3-D4
De Lairessestraat **E** A3-B3
De Ruijterkade **A** C1-D1
De Wittenkade **B** A4-B3
De Wittenstraat **B** A4-B3
Dijsselhofplantsoen
  E A3-A4
Dirk Van Hasseltssteeg
  A B2, **B** D5
Droogbak **A** B1, **B** D4
Egelantiersgr. **B** B5
Elandsgracht **C** A3-B2
Entrepotdok **F** B2-C3
Entrepotdoksluis **F** B3
Fagelstraat **B** A4-B4
Falckstraat **D** B4
Ferdinand Bolstr. **E** D2-D4
Fokke Simonszstraat
  C D5, **D** A4-B4, **E** D1-E1
Frans Halsstraat **E** D2-D3
Frederik Hendrikstraat
  B A4-A5
Frederiksplein **D** C4, **E** F1
Funenkade **F** C3
Gabriël Metsustr. **E** B2-C2
Gapersteeg **C** D2
Gasthuismolensteeg
  B C6, **C** C2
Gebed Zonder End **A** B5
Gedempte Begijnensloot
  A A5-A4, **C** C2-C3
Geldersekade **A** C3-D2
Gerard Terborgstraat **E** C3
Gerard Doustraat **E** D2-F2
Gevleweg **B** B1

Goudsbloemstraat
  B B4-C4
Gravenstr. **A** B3, **B** D6
Grimburgwal **A** B5
Groenburgwal **A** C5
Haarlemmer Houttuinen
  B B3-C3
Haarlemmer Houttuinen
  Droogbak **B** C3-D4
Haarlemmerdijk **B** C3
Haarlemmerplein **B** B3
Haarlemmerstraat
  A A1-B1, **B** C4-D4
Haarlemmerweg **B** A3-B3
Halvemaansbrug **A** B6
Halvemaansteeg
  A B6, **D** B2
Handelstraat **E** B4
Harmoniehof **E** C3-C4
Hartenstraat **C** B2-C2
Hasse-Laers Stg. **A** C2
Heiligeweg **A** A5,
  C C3-D3
Heinzestraat **E** A3-B3
Hembrugstraat **B** A1
Hemonystraat **E** F2
Hendrik Jonkerplein **B** C3
Henri Polaklaan **F** A3-B3
Henrick De Keijserplein
  E F3-F4
Henrick De Keijserstraat
  E E3
Henriette Ronnerpl. **E** F4
Herengracht **A** A6-C6,
  A A3-B1, **B** C6-D6,
  C C1-D4, **D** A2-C2
Herenstraat **A** A2, **B** C5
Hobbemakade
  C B6-C6, **E** C4-C1
Hobbemastraat
  C B6, **E** C1-C2
Hogesluisbrug **D** C4-D4
Hollandsetuin **B** C3
Honthorststraat
  C B6, **E** B1-C2
Hortusplantsoen **D** D2
Houtmankade **B** B2-C2
Houtrijkstraat **B** A1-B1

Index of streets, monuments, and places to visit

Huddekade **D** D4
Huidekoperstraat **D** B4
Huidenstraat **C** B3-C3
Ij Tunnel **F** A1-B1
Jacob Obrechtplein **E** B3
Jacob Obrechtstr. **E** A2-B3
Jacob Van Lennepkade **C** A3-A4
Jan Luijkenstraat **E** C1-B2
Johan M. Coenenstraat **E** B3-C3
Johan Vermeerstraat **E** C2-C3
Jozef Israëlskade **E** D4-F4
Kadijksplein **F** B2
Kalkmarkt **F** A2
Kalverstraat **A** A4-B6
Kattenburgergracht **F** B2
Kattenburgerkade **F** B2-C2
Kattenburgerkruisstraat **F** B2-C2
Kattenburgerplein **F** B2
Kattenburgerstr. **F** B2-C2
Kattengat **B** D4-D5
Keizerrijk **A** A4, **B** C6, **C** C2
Keizersgracht **A** A1-A2, **B** C4-B6, **C** C1-D4, **D** A2-C2
Kerkstraat **C** B4-D5, **D** A3-C3, **E** E1-F1
Kloveniersburgwal **A** C4-B5, **D** B1
KNSM Laan **F** E1-F1
Koestraat **A** C4
Koningsstraat **A** D4
Koningsplein **A** A5-A6
Korte's-Gravesandestr. **F** B4
Korte Amstelstraat **D** D3
Korte Keizersstraat **A** D4
Korte Leidsedwarsstraat **C** B4-C5
Korte Regulierdwarsstr. **D** B2
Kromme Waal **A** D3
Kuiperssteeg **A** B5
Kuipersstraat **E** F3
Lange Leidsedwarsstraat **C** B4-C5
Langestraat **A** A2, **B** C5-D5
Lastageweg **A** D3

Lauriergracht **C** A2-B2
Leidsegracht **C** A4-C3
Leidsekade **C** A4-B4
Leidsekruisstraat **C** B4-B5
Leidseplein **C** B4
Leidsestraat **C** B4-C3
Leliegracht **B** C5
Lijnbaansgracht **B** A6-B3, **C** A1-D6, **D** A-B4, **E** C1-E1
Lindengracht **B** B4-C4
Lindenstraat **B** B4-C4
Linnaeusstraat **F** C4
Looiersgracht **C** A3-B3
Maesstraat **E** C2
Manegestraat **D** D2
Marinierskade **F** C2
Marnixkade **B** A5-B3
Marnixplein **B** B5
Marnixstraat **B** A6-B3, **C** A1-B3
Martelaarsgracht **A** B2-C2, **B** D4-D5
Mauritskade **D** D4-F3, **F** A4-C3
Max Euweplein **C** B5
Mesdagstraat **E** E4
Mozartkade **E** C2
Mozes En Aäronstr. **A** A3-B3, **B** D6, **C** D1
Mr. Visserplein **D** C1-D1
Muiderpoort **F** B3
Muiderstraat **D** D1-D2
Muntplein **A** B6, **D** A2
Museumplein **E** B2-C2
Nassaukade **B** A6-B3, **C** A3-A4
Nassauplein **B** B3
Nes **A** B5-B4, **B** D6, **C** D2-D3
Nicolaas Maesstraat **E** A3-C2
Nicolaas Witsenkade **D** A4-B4, **E** D2-F2
Nieuwe Achtergracht **D** D3-E3
Nieuwe Amstelstraat **D** C2
Nieuwe Brugsteeg **A** C2
Nieuwe Doelenstr. **A** B5
Nieuwe Herengracht **D** C2-D2
Nieuwe Hoogstr. **A** C4
Nieuwe Keizersgracht **D** C2-D2, **F** A3

Nieuwe Kerkstraat **D** C3-E2, **F** A3
Nieuwe Leliestraat **B** B5
Nieuwe Prinsengracht **D** D3-F3, **F** A3
Nieuwe Ridderstraat **A** D3-D4
Nieuwe Spiegelstraat **C** C4-C5
Nieuwe Weteringstr. **C** C5
Nieuwe Westerdokstraat **B** C3-D4
Nieuwedoelenstraat **D** A1-B1
Nieuwendijk **A** B1-B3, **B** D6-D5
Nieuwevaart **F** B2
Nieuwewagenstraat **B** B3-C3
Nieuwezijds Armsteeg **A** B2-C2, **B** D5
Nieuwezijds Kolk **A** B2, **B** D5
Nieuwezijds Voorburgwal **A** A5-B2, **B** C6-D5
Nieuwmarkt **A** C4-D4
Niezel **A** C3
Noorderkerkstraat **B** C4
Noordermarkt **B** C4
Noorderstraat **C** D5, **D** A3-B3, **E** E1
Onbekendegracht **D** D3
Oosteinde **D** C4, **E** F1-F2
Oostenburgergracht **F** C3
Oosterdokskade **A** D2-D3, **F** A1
Oostelijke Handelskade **F** D2
Oude Brugsteeg **A** B2-C3
Oude Doelenstraat **A** B4-C4
Oude Hoogstr. **A** C4, **F** A2
Oude Looiersstr. **C** A3-B3
Oude Turfmarkt **A** B5
Oude Waal **A** D3, **F** A2
Oudekerkspl. **A** C3
Oudeman-Huispoort **A** B5
Oudeschans **A** D4
Oudezijds Voorburgwal **A** C3-B5, **B** D6
Oudezijds Achterburgwal **A** B5-C3

Overhaalsgang **F** B2-B3
Overtoom **C** A4-A5, **E** A1
Paardenstraat **D** B2
Paleisstraat **A** A4-B4, **B** C6-D6, **C** C2-D2
Palmgracht **B** B4-C3
Panamalaan **F** D3
Passeerdersgracht **C** A3-B3
Paulus Potterstraat **C** A6-B6, **E** B2-C1
Peperstraat **F** A2
Piet Heinkade **F** B1-D2
Pieter Aertszstraat **E** F3
Pieter Cornelisz Hooftstraat **C** A6, **E** B1
Pieter Jacobzstraat **A** B4, **B** D6
Pieter Lodewijk Taskstraat **E** F4
Pijlsteeg **A** B4, **B** D6
Planciusstraat **B** C2-C3
Plantage Kerklaan **F** A3-B3
Plantage Middenlaan **D** E2-F2, **F** A3-B3
Plantage Muidergracht **D** E2-F3, **F** A3-B3
Polonceaukade **B** A3
Prins Hendrikkade **A** B1-D3, **F** A2-B2
Prinsengracht **A** A1, **B** B6-C3, **C** B1-D5, **D** A3-C3, **E** D1-F1
Prinsenstraat **B** C4-C5
Prinseneiland **B** C3
Professor Tulppplein **D** D4
Raadhuisstraat **A** A3, **B** C5-C6, **C** C1
Raamgracht **A** C5
Raamplein **C** A4
Raamstraat **C** A4-B4
Rapenburg **F** A2
Rapenburgerplein **F** A2
Rapenburgerstr. **F** A2-A3
Realengracht **B** C2
Reestraat **B** B6, **C** B2
Reguliersbreestraat **A** B6, **D** A2-B2
Reguliersdwarsstraat **A** A6-B6, **C** C3-D4, **D** B2
Reguliersgracht **D** B2-B4, **E** E1